11+ Super Selective Maths: 30 Advanced Questions

Book 2

The 11+ Company

Published by The 11+ Company
34 Priory Road
Richmond
TW9 3DF
UNITED KINGDOM

Telephone: +44 (0)20 3667 3600
Email: enquiries@the11pluscompany.co.uk
Website: www.the11pluscompany.co.uk

First published in Great Britain in 2014.
Text, Cover Design and Illustrations Copyright © The 11+ Company 2014. All rights reserved, including translation.

The moral rights of the Author have been asserted in accordance with the Copyright, Design and Patents Act 1988.

ISBN: 978-0-9928958-1-5

British Library Cataloguing in Publication Data
A CIP catalogue record for this book is available from the British Library.

Contributors:

Text by Cavelle Creightney, PhD

Cover Design, Page Layout & Editing by Spiffing Covers

Subject Specialist Editing by Richard E. Martin, PhD Eng.

About This Book

The **11+ Super Selective MATHS** series has been written especially for children who seek 'more than ordinary' mathematical challenges. Filled with questions designed to stimulate thinking rather than simply elicit learned responses, this series provides the challenge that able pupils seek. Selective UK secondary schools are increasingly developing entrance exams that test potential rather than coached learning. As such we do not offer any particular exam format (e.g. CEM Durham, GL Assessment). Instead children's learning will be brought to life by our questions that demand insight and grasp of the fundamental concepts underlying each problem. Our fully worked answers demonstrate different strategies for solving 11+ mathematical challenges. Attractively designed and with ample space inside for pupils to express their working, this series will lead pupils to discover the fun, beauty and elegance of Mathematics!

There are three books in the **11+ Super Selective MATHS** series. Each book
- Contains 30 stimulating numerical and mathematical reasoning challenges
- Provides advanced practice material in mathematical thinking at 11+
- Includes fully worked answers & explanations
- Is suitable for use at the very top of Key Stage 2 and at Key Stage 3
- Is suitable for practice for scholarship exams and at 13+

About Our Authors
All our authors are highly qualified graduates and subject specialists from leading UK universities.

Question 31

(a) In base 10 arithmetic a number written as 673 means that there are 6 **hundreds**, 7 **tens** and 3 **units**:

673 (base 10) = (6 × **100**) + (7 × **10**) + (3 × **1**)

In base 10 arithmetic we use all the digits from 0 to 9.

We can also write numbers in base 5 which means that instead of the columns representing hundreds, tens and units, they now represent twenty-fives, fives and units.

For example, in base 5 the number 421 represents 4 **twenty-fives**, 2 **fives** and 1 **unit**:

421 (base 5) = (4 × **25**) + (2 × **5**) + (1 × **1**) = 100 + 10 + 1 = 111 (base 10)

In base 5 arithmetic only the digits 0, 1, 2, 3 and 4 are used.

Convert the following numbers, given in base 5, to base 10.

23 (base 5) = _____ (base 10)

312 (base 5) = _____ (base 10)

420 (base 5) = _____ (base 10)

(b) We can also write numbers in base 6. For example, in base 6 the number 531 represents 5 **thirty-sixes**, 3 **sixes** and 1 **unit**:

531 (base 6) = (5 × **36**) + (3 × **6**) + (1 × **1**) = 180 + 18 + 1 = 199 (base 10)

In base 6 arithmetic only the digits 0, 1, 2, 3, 4 and 5 are used.

Convert the following numbers, given in base 6, to base 10.

52 (base 6) = _____ (base 10)

435 (base 6) = _____ (base 10)

144 (base 6) = _____ (base 10)

(c) It is also possible to work backwards to convert numbers written in base 10 to either base 5 or base 6.

For example we can convert 65 from base 10 to base 5 in the following manner:

65 (base 10) = 50 + 15 + 0 = (2 × **25**) + (3 × **5**) + (0 × **1**) = 230 (base 5)

We can also convert 65 from base 10 to base 6 using a similar process:

65 (base 10) = 36 + 24 + 5 = (1 × **36**) + (4 × **6**) + (5 × **1**) = 145 (base 6)

Therefore 65 (base 10) = 230 (base 5) or 145 (base 6).

(i) Use this process to convert the following numbers from base 10 to base 5.

41 (base 10) = _____ (base 5)

163 (base 10) = _____ (base 5)

(ii) Use a similar process to convert the following numbers from base 10 to base 6.

41 (base 10) = _____ (base 6)

163 (base 10) = _____ (base 6)

Question 32

A cricket match lasts five days and Jane and Lucy sold lemonade throughout the entire match. At the end of the second day Lucy had sold all of the lemonade sold so far. During the remaining three days Jane and Lucy sold the same amount of lemonade. At the end of the five-day match Lucy had sold 85% of all the lemonade sold. What proportion of all the lemonade sold throughout the match was sold during the last three days of the match?

Answer: _____

Question 33

(a) A square crate with sides 60 cm on the **inside** contains 85 12-cm cubes. How many more 12-cm cubes are needed to completely fill the crate?

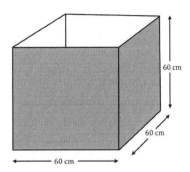

Answer: _____

(b) Ian uses 1-cm thick slabs of wood to construct a rectangular wooden crate whose **external dimensions** are 16 cm × 8 cm with a height of 7 cm (*shown below – not drawn to scale*). How many 2-cm cubes are needed to completely fill Ian's crate?

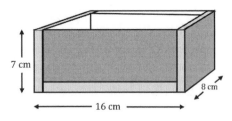

Answer: _____

Question 34

Kieran cuts out **three equilateral triangles** and arranges them into the figure shown below (*not drawn to scale*). The perimeters of the triangles A, B and C are in the ratio of 2:3:4 respectively. The length of one of the sides of triangle B is shown below. 1/3 of the length of one side of triangle B lies along a section of one side of triangle C. What is the total perimeter of the figure?

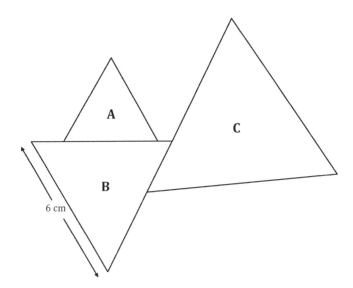

Answer: _____

Question 35

Maria has 5 cards with the following symbols.

   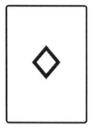 

Each symbol represents a number which is written on the reverse side of the card. Maria writes down the following facts about these numbers using their symbols:

$$\diamondsuit \; + \; \heartsuit \; = \; \blacksquare \; + \; \spadesuit$$

$$\varbigcirc \; + \; \varbigcirc \; = \; \heartsuit$$

$$\spadesuit \; + \; \heartsuit \; = \; \varbigcirc \; + \; \diamondsuit$$

$$\heartsuit \; + \; \varbigcirc \; \text{is not equal} \; \spadesuit \; + \; \varbigcirc$$

Write down the answer to the following questions using symbols. **Each answer must be expressed in only one symbol.**

(a)
$$\heartsuit \; + \; \varbigcirc \; ?$$

Answer: _____

(b)
$$\spadesuit \; + \; \varbigcirc \; ?$$

Answer: _____

Question 36

(a) A block of wood in the shape of a cube measures 25 cm along each edge. Charlie wants to cut it into 125 pieces with each piece being a 5-cm cube. What is the smallest number of cuts Charlie has to make? **Assume that Charlie is able to keep the shape held together while making cuts (for instance by using clamps).**

Answer: _____

(b) What if Charlie can't keep the shape held together while cutting. What is the smallest number of cuts he would then have to make?

Answer: _____

(c) The total surface area of the original block of wood is 6 × 25 cm × 25 cm = 3,750 cm². What is the total surface area of the 125 pieces?

Answer: _____

Question 37

Bruno cycles from Toytown to Tinseltown. He covers 7/15 of the total distance in the first hour and 1/3 of the total distance in the second hour. He takes one hour to complete the rest of the journey. His average speed for the first two hours was 15 km/hour. What was Bruno's average speed over the entire journey?

Answer: _____

Question 38

Tap A takes 4 minutes to fill a 1 litre jug. Tap B takes 4 minutes to fill a 1,200 ml jug.

(a) How long will Tap A take to completely fill the 1,200ml jug?

Answer: _____

(b) How long will Tap B take to fill the 1 litre jug 2/3 of the way?

Answer: _____

Question 39

(a) In the picture below, the number in each box is the sum of the numbers in the two boxes directly underneath. What is the value of **X**?

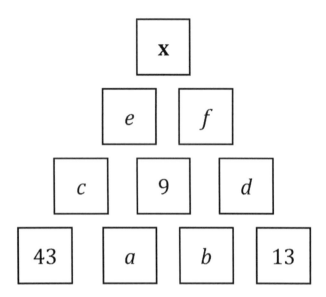

Answer: _____

(b) You are given six cards with the values 1, 2, 3, 4, 5 and 6 respectively.

Arrange the six cards so that the sum below is correct.

(c) Using **any digit from 0 to 9**, fill in the missing digits so that the sum below is correct. **You may use the same digit more than once**.

$$\square\,\square\,\square\,\square \times 6\,\square = 6\;2\;1\;2\;4$$

Question 40

Let n represent the **position** of numbers in a sequence.

$5n + 2$ is a **rule** for generating each **number** in the sequence according to its **position** in the sequence.

For example, when n = 1 this rule tells us that the **first number** in the sequence is 7, since $(5 \times 1) + 2 = 7$; when n = 2, this rule tells us that the **second number** in the sequence must be 12, since $(5 \times 2) + 2 = 12$; *and so on.*

(a) The following table gives **three rules** and their corresponding **sequences.** Complete each sequence by filling in the missing numbers in the table.

n	1	2	3	4	5	6	7	8	9
5n + 2	7	12	17	22	27	32			
3n + 4	7	10	13	16	19	22			
6n + 1	7	13	19	25	31	37			

(b) The following table shows **three sequences** however their **rules** are missing. Work out the rule that corresponds to each sequence and write your answers in the grey-shaded column on the left hand side. Complete each sequence by filling in the missing numbers in the table.

n	1	2	3	4	5	6	7	8	9
_____ ?	8	12	16	20	24	28			
_____ ?	9	17	25	33	41	49			
_____ ?	67	56	45	34	23	12			

Question 41

The figure below is made up of a square and four circles. The area of the square is 196 cm². The four corners of the square (W, X, Y and Z) lie at the centres of the four circles respectively. The area of each circle is $\pi \times r^2$, where $\pi = 22/7$.

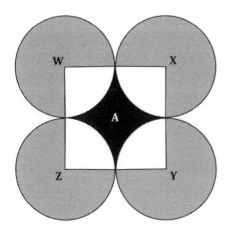

(a) Find the black-shaded area A.

Answer: _____

(b) The circumference of a circle is given by $2\pi r$, where $\pi = 22/7$. Use this to help you find **the sum of the perimeters of each of the** ¾ circles (*i.e.* the sum of the perimeters of each of the grey-shaded areas).

Answer: _____

Question 42

A solid wooden cube is painted red all around the outside. The cube is then cut into 27 smaller cubes of equal size. What fraction of the total surface area of all the new cubes will be red?

Answer: _____

Question 43

A cube has 6 faces with the numbers 1, 3, 5, 7, 9 and 11 written on them. Below are two views of the cube and its corresponding net. Some of the numbers are missing from the net. Fill in the missing numbers based on the two views of the cube. *Hint: to help you, try drawing the net on a separate piece of paper. Draw in as many faces as you can, cut it out and fold it into a cube. This should help you fill in any remaining blank faces more easily.*

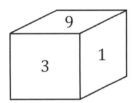   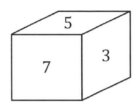

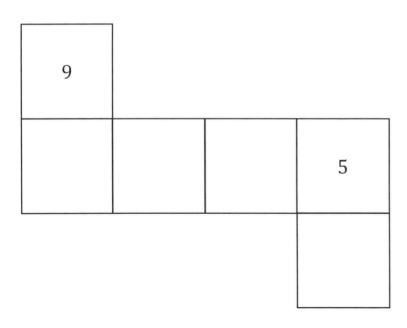

Question 44

Each of the symbols below has a value associated with it. No symbol has more than one value and no two symbols have the same value. You can add the values of all the symbols in any given row or column. This gives you the total value for that row or column and these total values are shown below.

✓	◇	◇		276
◉		◇	◇	340
✓	◇		◇	276
	◉	◉	✓	362
X	340	340	276	

Work out the value of each symbol and then find the value of **X**.

✓ = _____   ◇ = _____   ◉ = _____   X = _____

Question 45

(a) Crack the secret code to enter the dungeon where pirates have hidden their stolen treasure. You have to type the correct passcode into a keypad at the entrance of the dungeon. The passcode is the next number in the following sequence:

9,   19,   1119,   3119,   132119,   . . .

What is the passcode?

Answer: _____

(b) After their secret passcode has been discovered, the pirates change their secret code to **a sequence of eight numbers**. You found the **first seven numbers** of the sequence written on a piece of paper (aren't they careless!). Here are the first seven numbers:

13,   17,   31,   37,   71,   73,   79

What is the next (eighth) number in the sequence?

Answer: _____

(c) Having cracked their code once again, this time the pirates decide to get really smart. They place a guard at the entrance of the dungeon. As you approach, disguised as a memger of their gang, the guard shouts: 'Twelve! Six! Three!' - in that order and demands that you say **the next two elements in this new sequence**. As soon as you shout: 'One-and-a-half!' - the guard shouts: 'Wrong!' - but decides to offer you one last chance (since your disguise is very convincing). What do you now say in order to gain access to the dungeon?

Answer: _____

Question 46

You have three white coins with values 1, 2 and 3 respectively.

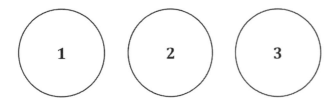

You also have three grey coins with values 1, 2 and 3 respectively and three black coins with values 1, 2 and 3 respectively.

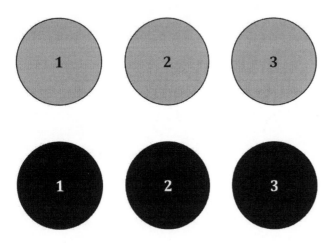

Arrange all your white, grey and black coins on the 3 × 3 grid below so that **no two coins of the same colour or same value lie next to each other (either above, below or to the left or right)**. *You may use the symbols W1, W2 and W3 to represent the white coins with values 1, 2 and 3 respectively; G1, G2 and G3 to represent the grey coins with values 1, 2 and 3 respectively; and B1, B2 and B3 to represent the black coins with values 1, 2 and 3 respectively.*

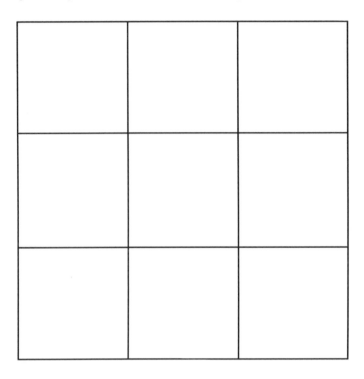

Question 47

The currency used on the strange island of Queb consists of 4 different kinds of bank notes called Naquebs, Baquebs, Vaquebs and Maquebs. Zeinab is going on holiday and must take each kind of currency with her, as it won't be possible to exchange them once she arrives. Her bank has given her a box containing 17 Naquebs, 14 Baquebs, 13 Vaquebs and 14 Maquebs. Without looking into the box, what is the smallest number of banknotes she must take out and take with her to make sure she has at least one of each type of note?

Answer: _____

Question 48

Claire creates the following number pattern by arranging numbers in order in a table.

	A	B	C	D	E	F	G	H	I
1	1	2	3	4	5	6	7	8	9
2	10	11	12	13	14	15	16	17	18
3	19	20	21	22	23	24	25	26	27
4									
5									
etc.									

She continues to add rows of numbers in the same way.

Suppose 2F means 'row 2, column F'.

(a) Which row and column will contain the following numbers?

Answers

139

256

97

683

756

(b) Which numbers will be found in each of the following rows and columns?

Answers

22F

73I

9B

17G

236A

Question 49

(a) Abe's Organic Farm sells 'organic boxes'. For every ½ kg of potatoes there must be 800 g of carrots and for every 600 g of carrots there must be 1.3 kg of meat. What is the ratio of vegetables (*i.e.* potatoes and carrots) to meat sold?

Answer: _____

(b) Brown's Dairy milk cartons are packed in crates of either 25 or 40. What is the smallest number of **full crates** required to pack exactly 690 milk cartons?

Answer: _____

(c) Joe's grocery store sells a total of 350 tins of beans throughout an entire week (7 days). Each day Joe sells 10 more tins than the day before. How many tins of beans does Joe sell on the **third** day of the week?

Answer: _____

(d) Lucy's corner shop sells 420 tins of tomatoes over an entire week (7 days). The ratio of tins sold on Monday to tins sold on Tuesday is 1:2; the ratio of tins sold on Tuesday to tins sold on Wednesday is 2:3; *and so on.* Lucy's sales pattern continues each day in a similar way. How many tins of tomatoes does Lucy sell on Friday?

Answer: _____

Question 50

(a) You are the leader of a summer holiday camp and you have to take three children (Anna, Joe and Peter) safely across a river, however the boat you have can only take two people at a time, including yourself. Anna and Joe always quarrel if they are left alone together and Joe and Peter always quarrel if left alone together. Describe in words how you would get all the children safely across the river without any quarrels.

Answer: _____

_____

_____

_____

_____

_____

(b) How many river crossings will you have made altogether?

Answer: _____

Question 51

Samuel takes four sheets of paper and folds each one in half. He then folds each one in half a second time and punches holes in them. In the pictures below the dotted lines show where the folds are and the circles show where the holes are. Draw where the holes will be when each sheet of paper is unfolded.

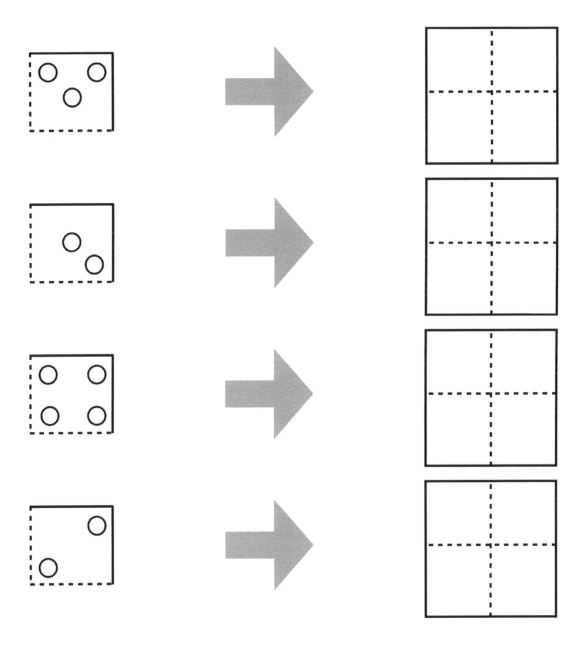

Question 52

Caroline's Grandfather is currently 3 times as old as Caroline. Ten years ago however he was 4 and 1/3 times as old as she was then. What was the sum of their ages 10 years ago?

Answer: _____

Question 53

(a) John cycles faster than Peter. For every hour they are both cycling John travels 1 km further than Peter. One day they both cycle the same distance from village A to village B. They start at the same time and John completes the journey in 6 hours while Peter completes the trip 2 hours later. Work out the speed at which Peter and John cycle and the distance between the two villages.

Answer: _____

(b) A third cyclist, Marie, leaves village A for village B at the same time that a fourth cyclist, James, leaves village B destined for village A. They cycle along the same road and James cycles 2 km/hour faster than Marie. (This means that for every hour of cycling James travels 2 km further than Marie). The two cyclists meet after they have cycled for 5 hours. What distance have they each travelled when they meet and what is Marie's average cycling speed?

Answer: _____

Question 54

Yosef needs to collect 17 tokens in order to swap them for a prize. Each week he collects four tokens but then gives away one of the tokens the following week.

(a) How many weeks does it take Yosef to collect 17 tokens?

Answer: _____

(b) How many tokens does he have left after he has received his prize?

Answer: _____

Question 55

You are given the following rules.

The rule for N_7 is 'add up the first 7 counting numbers'.

$$N_7 = 1 + 2 + 3 + 4 + 5 + 6 + 7 = 28$$

The rule for O_6 is 'add up the first 6 odd numbers'.

$$O_6 = 1 + 3 + 5 + 7 + 9 + 11 = 36$$

The rule for E_3 is 'add up the first 3 even numbers'.

$$E_3 = 2 + 4 + 6 = 12$$

(a) Complete the following table and describe any pattern you notice in the space below.

$O_1 =$	1	$= 1$	$= 1^2$
$O_2 =$	$1 + 3$	$= 4$	$= 2^2$
$O_3 =$	$1 + 3 + 5$	$= 9$	$= 3^2$
$O_4 =$			
$O_5 =$			
$O_6 =$			
$O_7 =$			
$O_8 =$			

Describe the pattern:_____

_____

_____

_____

_____

_____

(b) Work out the missing numbers **A**, **B**, **C** and **D** below.

$1 + 3 + 5 + \ldots + 77 = \mathbf{A}$

$1 + 3 + 5 + \ldots + 729 = \mathbf{B}$

$1 + 3 + 5 + \ldots + \mathbf{C} = 40,000$

$1 + 3 + 5 + \ldots + \mathbf{D} = 15,625$

A = _____   *B* = _____   *C* = _____   *D* = _____

(c) Work out the rule that connects E_n and N_n.

Answer: _____

(d) Re-write N_{10} in terms of O and E.

Answer: _____

(e) If $N_{10} = 55$, what is N_{11}?

Answer: _____

(f) Without using a calculator work out the value of N_{100}.

Answer: _____

(g) If $N_{301} = 45,451$, find the value of E_{150}.

Answer: _____

(h) You are told that $N_{505} = 127,765$. Work out the value of E_{250}.

Answer: _____

Question 56

(a) In the following number sequence, two numbers next to each other are multiplied to give the subsequent number. What are the missing values of this sequence?

____, ____,   1, ____, ____,   9, ____

(b) In this number sequence two numbers next to each other are also multiplied to give the subsequent number. Find the missing values of this sequence.

____, ____,   6, ____, ____,   24, ____

(c) This number sequence is made from **two rules** that **alternate** with each other. Identify both rules and fill in the missing values.

2,   4,   3,   6,   5,   10,   9,   ____,   ____,   ____

The rules are: _____

_____

_____

_____

(d) Identify the rule (or rules) that govern the following sequence and fill in the missing values.

0,   25,   7,   32,   5,   30,   ____,   ____,   ____

The rule is (or the rules are): _____

_____

_____

_____

Question 57

Joan has the following 5 cards.

 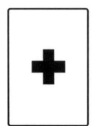   

Each card has one of the digits 2, 3, 4, 6 or 9 on the reverse side. No two cards have the same digit. Work out the value of each card from the relationships below.

♥ × ♥ = ⊕

◖ × ◖ = ✚◖

⊕ × ◉ = ✚◖

✚ × ♥ = 6

◖ = _____ ✚ = _____ ◉ = _____ ♥ = _____ ⊕ = _____

Question 58

Four boxes are made from pieces of square paper with each of the four corners cut off. Some of the dimensions are shown below (*not drawn to scale*).

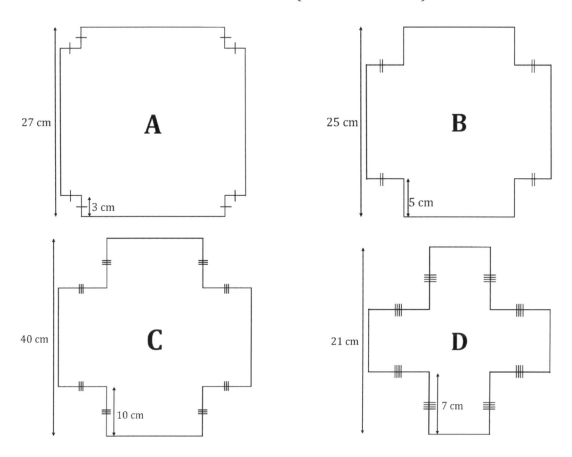

(a) Which of the four boxes has the greatest capacity?

Answer: _____

(b) How many 1-cm cubes are needed to fill the box with the smallest capacity?

Answer: _____

Question 59

(a) The red bag has three times as many balls as the green bag. The blue bag has four times as many balls as the red bag. The green bag therefore has how many times as many balls as the blue bag?

Answer: _____

(b) Three types of balls (black, white and coloured) are distributed among four boxes (green, red, blue and yellow). There are 96 balls in total. The coloured balls are distributed equally across the 4 boxes. There are 72 black and white balls in total and twice as many black balls as there are white balls. There are half as many white balls in the blue box as there are in total. There are three times as many white balls in total as there are black balls in the blue box. There are four times as many white balls in the red box as there are in the green box and fewer than three white balls in the yellow box. There are the same number of black balls in the green box as in the red box and twice as many in the yellow box.

(i) How many coloured balls are there in each of the four boxes?

Answer: _____

(ii) How many balls are there in total in each of the green, red, blue and yellow boxes?

Green box: _____ **Red box**: _____ **Blue box**: _____ **Yellow box**: _____

Question 60

At a wedding party each table seats 8 guests. 17 tables were initially ordered for 139 guests and then a further 27 tables were later ordered for an additional 223 guests.

(a) How many guests are still without seats?

Answer: _____

(b) How many more tables are required for all the guests to be seated?

Answer: _____

(c) It turns out that 31 guests are now unable to attend the wedding. How many tables will now be needed to ensure that all the remaining guests have a seat?

Answer: _____

(d) How many spare seats will there be?

Answer: _____

Answers

Answer 31

(a)
23 (base 5) = 2 **fives** + 3 **units** = 13 (base 10)

312 (base 5) = 3 **twenty-fives** + 1 **five** + 2 **units** =
82 (base 10)

420 (base 5) = 4 **twenty-fives** + 2 **fives** + 0 **units**
= 110 (base 10)

(b)
52 (base 6) = 5 **sixes** + 2 **units** = 32 (base 10)

435 (base 6) = 4 **thirty-sixes** + 3 **sixes** + 5 **units** =
167 (base 10)

144 (base 6) = 1 **thirty-six** + 4 **sixes** + 4 **units** =
64 (base 10)

(c)
(i) Remember: **In base 5 arithmetic only the
digits 0, 1, 2, 3 and 4 are used**!

41 (base 10) = 4 **tens** + 1 **unit** = 1 **twenty-five** + 3
fives + 1 **unit** = 131 (base 5)

163 (base 10) = 1 **hundred** + 6 **tens** + 3 **units** =
1 **hundred and twenty-five** + 1 **twenty-five** + 2
fives + 3 **units** = 1123 (base 5)

(ii) Remember: **In base 6 arithmetic only the
digits 0, 1, 2, 3, 4 and 5 are used**!

41 (base 10) = 4 **tens** + 1 **unit** = 1 **thirty-six** + 0
sixes + 5 **units** = 105 (base 6)

163 (base 10) = 1 **hundred** + 6 **tens** + 3 **units** = 4
thirty-sixes + 3 **sixes** + 1 **unit** = 431 (base 6)

Answer 32

At the end of the five-day match Lucy had sold
85% of all the lemonade sold throughout the
entire five days, so Jane must have sold 15% of all
the lemonade sold during the five days. However
Jane's lemonade was all sold during the last three
days and Jane sold the same amount of lemonade
as Lucy during this time, so this means that 30% of
all the lemonade sold must have been sold during
the last three days.

Answer 33

(a) A square crate with sides of 60 cm on the
inside can hold a total of 125 12-cm cubes. We can
imagine this visually as follows. The cubes will
be arranged in **layers** inside the crate. Each layer
will consist of 5 rows × 5 columns of cubes (*i.e.* 25
cubes) and there will be 5 such layers altogether.
Since the crate already contains 85 12-cm cubes it
will be possible to fit another 40 12-cm cubes to
completely fill the crate.

We can also work this out another way. The
volume (or **capacity**) of a 60-cm square crate is
60 cm × 60 cm × 60 cm = 216,000 cm^3. The volume
of a 12-cm cube is 12 cm × 12 cm × 12 cm = 1,728
cm^3. A 60-cm square crate can therefore hold
216,000 cm^3 ÷ 1,728 cm^3 = 125 12-cm cubes. If it
already has 85 12-cm cubes then it needs another
40 12-cm cubes to completely fill it.

(b) The base and each of the sides of the crate are
1 cm thick therefore, if the **external dimensions**
of the crate are 16 cm × 8 cm with an external
height of 7 cm, then the **internal dimensions** of
the crate must be 14 cm × 6 cm with an internal
height of 6 cm. The **internal capacity** (or **volume**)
of the crate is therefore 6 cm × 6 cm × 14 cm = 504
cm^3. However the volume of a 2-cm cube is 2 cm
× 2 cm × 2 cm = 8 cm^3 therefore the wooden crate
can hold 504 cm^3 ÷ 8 cm^3 = 63 2-cm cubes.

We can also think this through visually. Inside the
crate, along its base, is the first layer of 2-cm cubes
arranged in 7 rows × 3 columns. This makes a total
of 21 2-cm cubes along the base. Since the internal
height of the crate is 6 cm and each cube is a 2-cm
cube we will therefore have a total of 3 such layers
inside the crate. This makes a total of 21 × 3 = 63
2-cm cubes needed to fill the entire crate.

Answer 34

Triangle B has sides of 6 cm each. Since the triangles are equilateral and the perimeters are in the ratio of 2:3:4 then triangle A must have sides of 4 cm each and triangle C must have sides of 8 cm each. Since one complete side of triangle A lies along part of one side of triangle B, let a + b represent the length (in centimeters) of that side of triangle B that is left over. Also 1/3 of one side of triangle B lies along part of one side of triangle C and this length must be 2 cm. We can now establish the following measurements (in centimetres) throughout the whole figure:

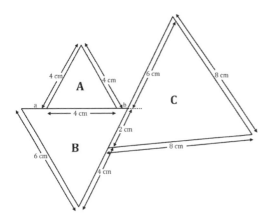

Since a and b must add up to 2 cm, then the total perimeter of the entire figure must equal 42 cm.

Answer 35

(a) If we combine the first two lines we get

$$\Diamond + \heartsuit + ☯ + ☯ = \heartsuit + ■ + ♠$$
_____ (A)

Let us call this equation (A).

From the third line we know that

$$♠ + \heartsuit = ☯ + \Diamond.$$

We can therefore eliminate

from the left hand side of equation (A) and

from the right hand side of equation (A). Equation (A) can therefore be simplified to

$$\heartsuit + ☯ = ■.$$

(b) This time if we combine the second and the third lines we get

$$♠ + \heartsuit + ☯ + ☯ = ☯ + \Diamond + \heartsuit$$
_____ (B)

Let us call this equation (B). In equation (B) we can eliminate

$$☯ + \heartsuit$$

from both sides of the equal sign and so equation (B) may be simplified to

$$♠ + ☯ = \Diamond.$$

Answer 36

(a) <u>If Charlie **can** keep the shape held together while making cuts:</u> The smallest number of cuts needed to produce 125 5-cm cubes is 12 cuts. These are represented by the dotted lines in the picture below.

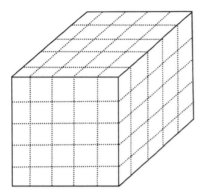

(b) <u>If Charlie **can't** keep the shape held together during the cutting</u>: His first four cuts would produce **5 slabs** of wood, each slab measuring 5 cm × 25 cm × 25 cm. He would subsequntly need to make four cuts to **each** of these 5 slabs which are 20 cuts in total and the result would now be a total of **25 batons,** each baton measuring 5 cm × 5 cm × 25 cm. To **each** of these 25 batons Charlie would now have to make 4 cuts which are 100 cuts in total. This would finally produce the 125 5-cm cubes (*i.e.* each measuring 5 cm × 5 cm × 5 cm). Adding up the total number of cuts Charlie would have to make if he can't hold the shape together gives us a total of 4 cuts + 20 cuts + 100 cuts = 124 cuts.

(c) Since each 5-cm cube has six sides, the total surface area of each of the 5-cm cubes must be 6 × 5 cm × 5 cm = 150 cm². Since there are 125 such cubes altogether the total surface area of the 125 cubes must be 125 × 150 cm² = 18,750 cm².

Answer 37

We were told that Bruno's average speed for the first 2 hours was 15 km/hour. This means that he must have covered a distance of 30 km in the first two hours and this distance represents 7/15 + 1/3 = 12/15 = 4/5 of the entire journey. If 30 km represent 4/5 of the entire journey then the total journey must have been 37½ km. Since Bruno completes the total journey of 37½ km in 3 hours then his average speed over the entire journey must have been 12 ½ km/hour.

Answer 38

(a) The rate of water flow from Tap A is 1 litre every 4 minutes. This is equivalent to 250 ml/minute. 50 ml would therefore take 60 seconds ÷ 5 = 12 seconds and 200 ml would therefore take 12 seconds × 4 = 48 seconds. Since Tap A takes 4 minutes to fill the 1 litre jug it would therefore take 4 minutes and 48 seconds to completely fill the 1,200 ml jug.

(b) The rate of water flow from Tap B is 1,200 ml every 4 minutes which equates to 300 ml/minute or 100 ml every 20 seconds. Tap B would therefore take 20 seconds × 10 = 200 seconds (which is the same as 3 minutes and 20 seconds) to completely fill the 1 litre jug. To fill the 1 litre jug 2/3 of the way would take 2/3 of that time which is 2 minutes and 13.3 seconds.

Answer 39

(a) **X** = $e + f = c + 9 + 9 + d = 43 + a + 18 + b + 13 = 43 + 18 + 13 + 9$ (since $a + b = 9$) = 83.

(b) Trying each digit in turn, place a single digit into the 3rd box and see what follows. *E.g.* <u>if we place the digit 1 into the 3rd box</u> we see that this can't be correct because whatever digit then goes into the 2nd box would have to be repeated in the 6th box and we can't use the same digit more than once. Now <u>try placing the digit 2 into the 3rd box</u>. With the digit 2 in the 3rd box try now placing each of the remaining digits, in turn, into the 2nd box and see what follows. We quickly see that there can be no solution that has the digit 2 in the 3rd box. <u>Continue like this trying each digit in turn in the third box.</u> You will see that the correct sum has to be:

| 5 | 4 | × | 3 | = | 1 | 6 | 2 |

(c) First note that 124 = 62 × 2, therefore 62,124 is easily divisible by 62 to give 1,002. The correct sum is therefore:

| 1 | 0 | 0 | 2 | × | 6 | 2 | = | 6 | 2 | 1 | 2 | 4 |

Answer 40

(a)

n	5n + 2	3n + 4	6n + 1
1	7	7	7
2	12	10	13
3	17	13	19
4	22	16	25
5	27	19	31
6	32	22	37
7	37	25	43
8	42	28	49
9	47	31	55

(b) Rules for sequences can be written in a general form as $an + b$, where n is the **position** of numbers in the sequence. $a + b$ always gives us the first number of the series (since n = 1) while a tells us how much we have to add to each number to get the subsequent number.

In the <u>first sequence</u> we add 4 to each number to get the next number in the sequence, therefore a = 4. Since the first number in the sequence is 8 it must be the case that b is also 4. The rule for the first sequence is therefore 4n + 4. The rule and the missing values for this sequence are shown in the first column of the table below.

In the <u>second sequence</u> we add 8 to each number to get the next number in the sequence therefore a = 8. Since the first number is 9 then this means that b must be 1 and the rule for the second sequnce must be 8n + 1. The rule and the missing values for this sequence are shown in the second column of the table below.

In the <u>third sequence</u> this time we **take away** 11 from each number to get the subsequent number, therefore a = −11. Since the first number in the sequence is 67 this means that b must be 78 (a + b = −11 + 78 = 67), therefore the rule for this sequence is −11n + 78. The rule and the missing values for this sequence are shown in the third column of the table below.

n	4n + 4	8n + 1	−11n + 78
1	8	9	67
2	12	17	56
3	16	25	45
4	20	33	34
5	24	41	23
6	28	49	12
7	32	57	1
8	36	65	-10
9	40	73	-21

Answer 41

(a) The black-shaded area A is equal to the area of the square *minus* the total area of the four white quadrants. Since the area of the square is 196 cm² then each side of the square must be 14 cm (since 14 cm × 14 cm = 196 cm²) and the radius of each circle must be 7 cm. The area of each of the quadrants is ¼ of the area of its respective circle, i.e. ¼ × (22/7 × 7 cm × 7 cm) = ¼ × 154 cm². The total area of the four quadrants is therefore 154 cm² and the shaded area A must therefore be 196 cm² − 154 cm² = 42 cm².

(b) The circumference of one of the circles is 2πr = 2 × 22/7 × 7 cm = 44 cm. The perimeter of one of the grey-shaded areas is therefore (¾ × the circumference) + 7 cm + 7 cm = 47 cm. The sum of the perimeters of all of the grey-shaded areas is therefore 47 cm × 4 = 188 cm.

Answer 42

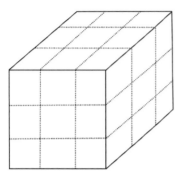

When the original cube is cut into 27 smaller cubes the result is **3 layers** of cubes with each layer consisting of 9 cubes. The 9 cubes in each layer are arranged in a 3 × 3 formation. Each of these smaller cubes has 6 sides and there are a total of 27 small cubes making a total of 27 × 6 sides = 162 sides and each side is of equal surface area. The original (large) cube had 6 sides and each side was partitioned into 9 (to create the 27 small cubes) so the number of sides that have red paint on them must be 9 × 6 = 54. Therefore the fraction of the total surface area of the 27 new cubes that are painted red must be 54/162 = 1/3.

Answer 43

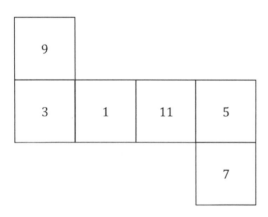

Answer 44

Note: a number next to a symbol tells us how many of that particular symbol we have. So 2◇ tells us we have '2 of ◇' which is the same as ◇ + ◇.

The following information can be established from the table:

$$2\diamondsuit + \checkmark = 276 \quad \underline{\qquad}(1)$$

$$2\diamondsuit + \circledcirc = 340 \quad \underline{\qquad}(2)$$

$$2\circledcirc + \checkmark = 362 \quad \underline{\qquad}(3)$$

We can use this information to find the values of

$\checkmark$, $\diamondsuit$ and $\circledcirc$.

First subtract equation (1) from equation (2). This gives us

$$\circledcirc - \checkmark = 64 \quad \underline{\qquad}(4)$$

which we can call equation (4). Add equation (4) to equation (3) and simplify to get

$$3\circledcirc = 426$$

or

$$\circledcirc = 142.$$

By substituting

$$\circledcirc = 142$$

into equation (2) we see that

$$\diamondsuit = 99.$$

We can now substitute

$$\diamondsuit = 99$$

into equation (1) to get

$\sqrt{} = 78$.

We can now use these results plus the information in the table to establish that

$\mathbf{X} = 2\sqrt{} + \bullet = 298$.

Summary of results

$\diamondsuit = 99$, $\sqrt{} = 78$, $\bullet = 142$, $\mathbf{X} = 298$

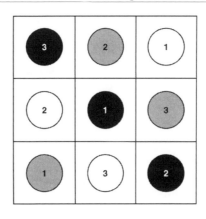

Answer 45

(a) 1113122119. Starting with the number nine, each subsequent number in the sequence describes the previous number. So our sequence is: nine; one "nine"; one "one", one "nine"; three "ones", one "nine"; one "three", two "ones", one "nine"; *etc.* The next number must therefore be: one "one", one "three", one "two", two "ones", one "nine".

(b) The next (eighth) number in this sequence is 97. The sequence is the sequence of **reversible prime numbers**. A **prime number** is 'a number that is divisible only by one and itself'. A **reversible prime number** is 'a prime number that produces another prime number when its digits are reversed'. The next number in the sequence is therefore 97.

(c) You say "five" – which is the number of letters in the preceding word - then "four" – which again is the number of letters in the preceding word.

Answer 46

The following is one possible arrangement. See if you can find other possibilities.

Answer 47

She must take at least 17 + 14 + 14 + 1 = 46 notes altogether.

Answer 48

First note that in this pattern there are 9 columns altogether. Column I is the ninth column and it always contains a multiple of 9, *i.e.* 9 × the corresponding 'row number'. If Claire continued the same pattern then she would get the following results.

(a)

Number	139	256	97	683	756
Row/Column	16D	29D	11G	76H	84I

(b)

Row/Column	22F	73I	9B	17G	236A
Number	195	657	74	151	2,116

Answer 49

(a) First convert all the weights to either grams or kilograms. We choose to work in grams so we will first convert all the given weights to grams. Since 1 kg = 1,000 g we may re-write the ratios as follows: for every 500 g of potatoes there are 800 g of carrots and for every 600 g of carrots there are

1,300 g of meat. This means that for every 600 g of carrots there will be 375 g of potatoes plus 1,300 g of meat. The ratio of vegetables (*i.e.* carrots plus potatoes) to meat must therefore be 975:1,300 which we can simplify as 3:4.

(b) To minimize the number of crates, first pack as many milk cartons as possible into the 40-carton crates. Note that 640 milk cartons can be packed into 16 crates (since 16 crates × 40 cartons per crate = 640 cartons). There are still 50 milk cartons remaining and these can be packed into 2 crates of 25 cartons each. So the smallest number of full crates required is 16 of the 40-carton crates **plus** 2 of the 25-carton crates which make 18 crates in total.

(c) Let X represent the number of tins of beans sold on day 1. On day 2 therefore Joe must have sold X + 10 tins; on day 3 he sells X + 20 tins; *and so on*. We can create a table like the one below to show how many tins of beans Joe sells on each day of the week:

Day	1	2	3	4	5	6	7
Number of tins sold	X	X + 10	X + 20	X + 30	X + 40	X + 50	X + 60

If we add up the number of tins sold each day we see that by the end of the week Joe must have sold a total of 7X + 210 tins of beans. Since this must be equal to 350 tins then 7X + 210 = 350 and X = 20. Since X is the number of tins sold on day 1, then Joe sold 20 tins on the first day. The number of tins sold each day can now be shown in the table below:

Day	1	2	3	4	5	6	7
Number of tins sold	20	30	40	50	60	70	80

On the third day we see that Joe must have sold 40 tins of beans.

(d) Let W be the number of tins of tomatoes Lucy sells on Monday. If 1:2 is the ratio of the number of tins sold on Monday to the number of tins sold on Tuesday, then it means that 2W is the number of tins sold on Tuesday. If 2:3 is the ratio of the number of tins sold on Tuesday to the number of tins sold on Wednesday, then it means that for every 2 tins Lucy sells on Tuesday she sells 3 tins on Wednesday, so 3W is the number of tins sold on Wednesday (since Lucy sold 2W on Tuesday). If we continue reasoning like this for every day of the week we see that the number of tins of tomatoes Lucy sells on any given day can be shown in a table like this:

Day	Monday	Tuesday	Wednesday	Thursday	Friday	Saturday	Sunday
Number of tins sold	W	2W	3W	4W	5W	6W	7W

We were told that the total number of tins of tomatoes sold over the whole week was 420, so this means that W + 2W + 3W + 4W + 5W + 6W + 7W = 28W = 420 which in turn means that W = 420 ÷ 28 = 15. Remember that W is the number of tins sold on Monday so Lucy sold 15 tins on Monday. The table shows that on Friday Lucy sold 5 times the number sold on Monday, so Lucy must have sold 15 tins × 5 = 75 tins of tomatoes on Friday.

Answer 50

(a) *An example answer*: "First I take Joe across the river. I leave Anna and Peter behind together as they won't quarrel with each other. I come back and take Anna across the river. When I return I bring Joe back with me since Anna and Joe quarrel if left alone together. I now take Peter across the river. I leave Anna and Peter alone together on the other side of the river while I come back for Joe."

An alternative answer: "First I take Joe across the river. I come back and take Peter across the river. When I return I bring Joe back with me. I now take Anna across the river. I leave Anna and Peter alone together on the other side of the river while I come back for Joe."

(b) Altogether you would have made a total of <u>seven river crossings</u>.

Answer 51

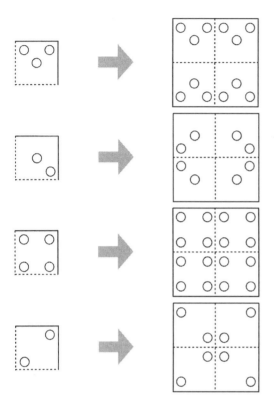

Answer 52

Let X represent Caroline's age now. Therefore 3X must be the age of her Grandfather today. Ten years ago Caroline's age was X – 10 and her grandfather's age was 3X – 10. We can organise all this information into a table like this:

	Caroline's age	Grandfather's age
Now	X	3X
Ten years ago	X – 10	3X – 10 = (4 + ⅓) × (X – 10)

From the information in the grey box we have $3X - 10 = (4 + 1/3) \times (X - 10) = (4 + 1/3)X - 130/3$. We can re-arrange this to get $130/3 - 10 = (4 + 1/3)X - 3X$. This is the same as $100/3 = 4X/3$ or $4X =$

100 or X = 25. If X = 25 then 3X = 75, X – 10 = 15 and 3X – 10 = 65. So ten years ago Caroline was 15 and her grandfather was 65. The sum of their ages at that time was therefore 80.

Answer 53

(a) For every hour they both cycle John travels 1 km further than Peter. When John completes the trip in 6 hours Peter, therefore, must still have another 6 km left to finish the trip. Since Peter completes these 6 km in 2 hours his cycling speed must have been 3 km/hour. Therefore John's cycling speed must have been 4 km/hour. The total distance between the two villages must therefore be 24 km (since John cycled 4 km/hour for 6 hours and Peter cycled 3 km/hour for 8 hours).

(b) After 5 hours of cycling James must have cycled 10 km further than Marie (5 hours × 2 km/hour = 10 km). Since the distance between the two villages is 24 km (we worked this out in part (a)) then James must have cycled 17 km while Marie must have cycled 7 km. If Marie cycles 7 km in 5 hours then her average speed must be 7 km ÷ 5 hours = 1.4 km/hour.

Answer 54

(a) The table below shows how many new tokens Yosef collects each week, how many he gives away each week (shown in italics) and how many he accumulates by the end of one week to carry forward to the next week.

Week	1	2	3	4	5	6
Tokens brought forward from previous week	0	4	7	10	13	16
Tokens given away	*0*	*1*	*1*	*1*	*1*	*1*
New tokens collected	4	4	4	4	4	4
Total number of tokens accumulated by the end of the week	4	7	10	13	16	19

This table shows that it takes Yosef 6 weeks to collect 17 tokens.

(b) Since Yosef actually collects 19 tokens by the end of week 6 he therefore has 2 tokens left over after he receives his prize.

Answer 55

(a) The completed table is shown below:

$O_1 =$	1	$= 1$	$= 1^2$
$O_2 =$	$1 + 3$	$= 4$	$= 2^2$
$O_3 =$	$1 + 3 + 5$	$= 9$	$= 3^2$
$O_4 =$	$1 + 3 + 5 + 7$	$= 16$	$= 4^2$
$O_5 =$	$1 + 3 + 5 + 7 + 9$	$= 25$	$= 5^2$
$O_6 =$	$1 + 3 + 5 + 7 + 9 + 11$	$= 36$	$= 6^2$
$O_7 =$	$1 + 3 + 5 + 7 + 9 + 11 + 13$	$= 49$	$= 7^2$
$O_8 =$	$1 + 3 + 5 + 7 + 9 + 11 + 13 + 15$	$= 64$	$= 8^2$

Describe the pattern: From the table we see that the sum of the first odd number is 1^2, the sum of the first 2 odd numbers is 2^2; the sum of the first 3 odd numbers is 3^2; *and so on*. We can make a guess that in general the sum of the first n odd numbers must be n^2.

(b) To find **A**, first notice that **A** is just the sum of a sequence of odd numbers. To find **A** we first need to work out the **number of odd numbers** in the sequence. The last number in the sequence is 77 so the number of odd numbers must be half of 78 which is 39, therefore **A is the sum of the first 39 odd numbers**. From our table in section (a) we know that the sum of the first 39 odd numbers must be 39^2, therefore **A** = 39^2 = 1,521.

We can follow a similar procedure to show that **B is the sum of the first 365 odd numbers** since there are 365 odd numbers in this sequence (note that 365 is half of 730 and 730 is number that follows 729). Therefore **B** = 365^2 = 133,225.

To find **C**, we reverse the procedure we used to find **A** and **B**. This time notice that 40,000 is the square of the number 200 (*i.e.* 200^2 = 40,000), so this tells us we must be adding up the first 200 odd numbers and **C must be the 200th odd number**. The 200th odd number is given by $(200 \times 2) - 1 =$ 399 therefore **C** = 399.

We can follow a similar procedure to find **D as the 125th odd number** (since 125^2 = 15,625). The 125th odd number is $(125 \times 2) - 1 = 249$ therefore **D** = 249.

Summary of results
A = 39^2 = 1,521
B = 365^2 = 133,225
C = 399
D = 249

(c) First choose a value for n, *e.g.* n = 5. Therefore we have $N_5 = 1 + 2 + 3 + 4 + 5$ and $E_5 = 2 + 4 + 6 + 8 + 10$ which is just the same as $2 \times N_5$. It's easy to see that this rule must be true no matter what actual value we take for n. Therefore our rule must be $E_n = 2 \times N_n$.

(d) $N_{10} = 1 + 2 + 3 + 4 + 5 + 6 + 7 + 8 + 9 + 10$. We can see that the sum of the first 10 counting numbers is made up of the sum of the first 5 odd numbers **plus** the sum of the first five even numbers. Therefore $N_{10} = O_5 + E_5$.

(e) $N_{11} = N_{10} + 11 = 55 + 11 = 66$.

(f) We can use the following relationships (which have been established in earlier parts of this question) to work out N_{100}:

$N_{100} = O_{50} + E_{50}$ (this follows from part (d))
In general: $N_n = O_{\frac{1}{2}n} + E_{\frac{1}{2}n}$
$O_n = n^2$ (part (a))
$E_n = 2 \times N_n$ (part (c))

Therefore,

N_{100}

$= O_{50} + E_{50}$

$= 50^2 + [2 \times N_{50}]$

$= 50^2 + [2 \times (O_{25} + E_{25})]$

$= 50^2 + [2 \times (25^2 + (2 \times N_{25}))]$

$= 50^2 + [2 \times (25^2 + (2 \times (25 + N_{24})))]$

$= 50^2 + [2 \times (25^2 + (2 \times (25 + O_{12} + E_{12})))]$

$= 50^2 + [2 \times (25^2 + (2 \times (25 + 12^2 + (2 \times N_{12}))))]$

$= 50^2 + [2 \times (25^2 + (2 \times (25 + 12^2 + (2 \times (O_6 + E_6)))))]$

$= 50^2 + [2 \times (25^2 + (2 \times (25 + 12^2 + (2 \times (36 + (2 \times N_6))))))]$

$= 50^2 + [2 \times (25^2 + (2 \times (25 + 12^2 + \mathbf{(2 \times (36 + (2 \times 21))))))]}$

$= 2{,}500 + [2 \times (625 + (2 \times (25 + 144 + \mathbf{156})))]$

$= 2{,}500 + [2 \times 1{,}275]$

$= 2{,}500 + 2{,}550$

$= 5{,}050.$

(g) First, re-write N_{301} as follows.

N_{301}

$= N_{300} + 301$

$= O_{150} + E_{150} + 301$

$= 150^2 + E_{150} + 301$

$= 22{,}500 + E_{150} + 301.$

Since $N_{301} = 45{,}451$, then $E_{150} = (45{,}451 - 22{,}500) - 301 = 22{,}650.$

(h) First, re-write N_{505} as follows.

N_{505}

$= N_{500} + 501 + 502 + 503 + 504 + 505$

$= O_{250} + E_{250} + 2{,}515$

$= 250^2 + E_{250} + 2{,}515$

$= 62{,}500 + 2{,}515 + E_{250}$

$= 65{,}015 + E_{250}.$

Since $N_{505} = 127{,}765$, then $E_{250} = 127{,}765 - 65{,}015 = 62{,}750.$

Answer 56

(a) <u>1/3</u>, <u>3</u>, 1, <u>3</u>, <u>3</u>, 9, <u>27</u>

(b) <u>18</u>, <u>1/3</u>, 6, <u>2</u>, <u>12</u>, 24, <u>288</u>

(c) Starting with the number 2, the two alternating rules are: 'multiply by 2 to get the next number, take away 1 to get the next number, multiply by 2 to get the next number, take away 1 to get the next number, *and so on*. The completed sequence is 2, 4, 3, 6, 5, 10, 9, <u>18</u>, <u>17</u>, <u>34</u>.

(d) Starting with 0, the rules are: 'add 25 to get the next number, add the digits of that number to get the next number, add 25 to get the next number, add the digits of that number to get the next number, *and so on*. The completed sequence is 0, 25, 7, 32, 5, 30, <u>3</u>, <u>28</u>, <u>10</u>.

Answer 57

You may use your knowledge of square numbers to help you work out the value of each card. The only possible values for each card are 2, 3, 4, 6 and 9. Therefore, since

$$\text{◕} \times \text{◕} = \text{✚◕}$$

then it must be the case that

$$\text{◕} = 6$$

and

$$\text{✚} = 3.$$

Since

✚ = 3

then we must have

♥ = 2.

Since

♥ × ♥ = ⊕

this implies that

⊕ = 4.

Finally, since

⊕ × ◉ = ✚◖

then

◉ = 9.

Summary of results

♥ = 2
◖ = 6
⊕ = 4
◉ = 9
✚ = 3

Answer 58

(a) The capacities of the four boxes are shown below:

Capacity of Box A
21 cm × 21 cm × 3 cm = 1,323 cm³

Capacity of Box B
15 cm × 15 cm × 5 cm = 1,125 cm³

Capacity of Box C
20 cm × 20 cm × 10 cm = 4,000 cm³

Capacity of Box D
7 cm × 7 cm × 7 cm = 343 cm³

Therefore box C has the largest capacity.

(b) The box with the smallest capacity is box D with a capacity of 343 cm³. This means that 343 1-cm cubes will be needed to fill this box.

Answer 59

(a) For every ball in the green bag there are 3 balls in the red bag and 12 balls in the blue bag. Therefore the green bag has 1/12 of the number of balls in the blue bag.

(b) It's best to first create a table such as the one below and carefully organize all the information provided. You can then check to see that the following must be true:

	Black Balls	White Balls	Coloured Balls	Total Number of Balls
Green Box	10	2	6	18
Red Box	10	8	6	24
Blue Box	8	12	6	26
Yellow Box	20	2 (< 3)	6	28
Total Number of Balls	48	24	24	96

(i) There are 6 coloured balls in each of the 4 boxes.

(ii) There are 18 balls in total in the green box, 24 in the red box, 26 in the blue box and 28 in the yellow box.

Answer 60

(a) A total of 17 + 27 = 44 tables were ordered. Each table seats 8 guests so a total of 44 tables × 8 seats per table = 352 seats are available. However there are 139 + 223 = 362 guests altogether therefore 10 guests are still without seats.

(b) 2 more tables are required to seat the remaining 10 guests.

(c) If 31 guests do not attend that leaves 362 − 31 = 331 guests who still need seats. Each table seats 8 guests. 331 ÷ 8 = 41 remainder 3, therefore 42 tables will be required.

(d) There will be 5 spare seats.

Printed in Great Britain
by Amazon.co.uk, Ltd.,
Marston Gate.